50 Japanese Night Recipes for Home

By: Kelly Johnson

Table of Contents

- California Sushi Rolls
- Ramen Noodle Soup
- Teriyaki Chicken
- Tempura Vegetables
- Miso Soup
- Yakitori Skewers
- Tonkatsu Pork Cutlets
- Okonomiyaki Pancakes
- Gyoza Dumplings
- Katsu Curry
- Chirashi Sushi Bowl
- Udon Noodle Stir-Fry
- Soba Noodle Salad
- Oyakodon Chicken and Egg Rice Bowl
- Takoyaki Octopus Balls
- Sashimi Platter
- Karaage Fried Chicken
- Japanese Curry Rice
- Yaki Udon Stir-Fry
- Oden Hot Pot
- Nikujaga Beef and Potato Stew
- Sukiyaki Beef Hot Pot
- Onigiri Rice Balls
- Tofu Teriyaki
- Hiyayakko Cold Tofu
- Tonjiru Pork Miso Soup
- Ebi Fry Shrimp
- Chawanmushi Steamed Egg Custard
- Zaru Soba Cold Buckwheat Noodles
- Nasu Dengaku Miso-glazed Eggplant
- Ankake Yakisoba
- Kakiage Tempura Bowl
- Tamago Sushi
- Tori Nanban Fried Chicken with Tartar Sauce
- Hiya Yakko Chilled Tofu

- Shabu-Shabu Hot Pot
- Somen Noodle Salad
- Yudofu Hot Tofu
- Buta no Kakuni Braised Pork Belly
- Kabocha Korokke Pumpkin Croquettes
- Ochazuke Rice with Tea
- Chuka Kurage Japanese Marinated Jellyfish Salad
- Kani Salad Crab Salad
- Age Dashi Tofu
- Yaki Onigiri Grilled Rice Balls
- Ebi Mayo Shrimp with Spicy Mayo
- Hamachi Kama Grilled Yellowtail Collar
- Katsudon Pork Cutlet Rice Bowl
- Tsukemono Japanese Pickles
- Natto Fermented Soybeans

California Sushi Rolls

Ingredients:

- Sushi rice
- Nori seaweed sheets
- Imitation crab meat (or real crab if available)
- Avocado
- Cucumber
- Sesame seeds (optional)
- Soy sauce, for serving
- Pickled ginger, for serving
- Wasabi, for serving

Instructions:

1. Cook sushi rice according to package instructions. Let it cool to room temperature.
2. Prepare your filling ingredients: slice the avocado and cucumber into thin strips.
3. Lay a sheet of nori seaweed on a bamboo sushi mat.
4. Spread a thin layer of sushi rice evenly over the nori, leaving about 1 inch of space at the top edge.
5. Place the imitation crab meat, avocado slices, and cucumber strips horizontally across the center of the rice.
6. Using the bamboo mat, roll the nori and rice tightly around the filling. Apply gentle pressure to ensure the roll holds its shape.
7. Seal the roll by moistening the top edge of the nori with a bit of water.
8. If desired, sprinkle sesame seeds over the top of the roll and gently press them into the rice.
9. Use a sharp knife to slice the roll into bite-sized pieces.
10. Serve the California Roll with soy sauce, pickled ginger, and wasabi on the side.

Enjoy your homemade California Rolls!

Ramen Noodle Soup

Ingredients:

- 4 cups chicken or vegetable broth
- 2 packs of instant ramen noodles (discard the seasoning packets or save for another use)
- 2 cups thinly sliced vegetables (such as carrots, mushrooms, bok choy, and green onions)
- 2 boiled eggs, halved
- 1 cup cooked protein (such as shredded chicken, cooked shrimp, tofu, or pork)
- Soy sauce, to taste
- Sesame oil, to taste
- Sriracha or chili garlic sauce, to taste (optional)
- Fresh cilantro and sliced green onions, for garnish
- Sesame seeds, for garnish

Instructions:

1. In a large pot, bring the chicken or vegetable broth to a simmer over medium heat.
2. Add the sliced vegetables to the broth and let them cook until tender, about 5-7 minutes.
3. While the vegetables are cooking, prepare the instant ramen noodles according to the package instructions. Drain and set aside.
4. Once the vegetables are tender, add the cooked protein of your choice to the pot and heat through.
5. Season the broth with soy sauce, sesame oil, and Sriracha or chili garlic sauce, adjusting to taste.
6. Divide the cooked ramen noodles among serving bowls.
7. Ladle the hot broth and vegetables over the noodles.
8. Top each bowl with a halved boiled egg.
9. Garnish with fresh cilantro, sliced green onions, and sesame seeds.
10. Serve immediately and enjoy your comforting bowl of homemade ramen noodle soup!

Feel free to customize your ramen noodle soup with additional toppings such as nori seaweed, corn kernels, bean sprouts, or bamboo shoots.

Teriyaki Chicken

Ingredients:

- 4 boneless, skinless chicken breasts
- 1/2 cup soy sauce
- 1/4 cup mirin (Japanese sweet rice wine)
- 2 tablespoons honey or brown sugar
- 2 cloves garlic, minced
- 1 teaspoon grated ginger
- 2 tablespoons vegetable oil
- Sesame seeds, for garnish (optional)
- Sliced green onions, for garnish (optional)

Instructions:

1. In a bowl, mix together the soy sauce, mirin, honey or brown sugar, minced garlic, and grated ginger to make the teriyaki sauce.
2. Place the chicken breasts in a shallow dish or resealable plastic bag and pour half of the teriyaki sauce over them. Reserve the other half of the sauce for later.
3. Marinate the chicken in the refrigerator for at least 30 minutes, or up to 2 hours, turning occasionally to ensure even coating.
4. Heat the vegetable oil in a large skillet or grill pan over medium-high heat.
5. Remove the chicken from the marinade and discard the marinade.
6. Cook the chicken in the hot skillet for 6-8 minutes per side, or until cooked through and golden brown on the outside. The internal temperature should reach 165°F (75°C).
7. While the chicken is cooking, pour the reserved teriyaki sauce into a small saucepan and bring it to a simmer over medium heat. Let it cook for 2-3 minutes, stirring occasionally, until slightly thickened.
8. Once the chicken is cooked, remove it from the skillet and let it rest for a few minutes.
9. Slice the chicken breasts into strips or serve them whole.
10. Drizzle the cooked teriyaki sauce over the chicken.
11. Garnish with sesame seeds and sliced green onions, if desired.
12. Serve the teriyaki chicken with steamed rice and your favorite vegetables for a delicious meal.

Enjoy your homemade teriyaki chicken!

Tempura Vegetables

Ingredients:
- Assorted vegetables (such as bell peppers, zucchini, sweet potatoes, mushrooms, broccoli, and green beans)
- 1 cup all-purpose flour
- 1/2 cup cornstarch
- 1 teaspoon baking powder
- 1 cup ice-cold water
- Vegetable oil, for frying
- Salt, to taste
- Dipping sauce (such as soy sauce, tempura sauce, or ponzu sauce), for serving

Instructions:

1. Prepare the vegetables by washing them thoroughly and cutting them into bite-sized pieces or strips.
2. In a large mixing bowl, combine the all-purpose flour, cornstarch, and baking powder.
3. Gradually add the ice-cold water to the dry ingredients, whisking until the batter is smooth. Be careful not to overmix; a few lumps are okay.
4. Heat vegetable oil in a deep fryer or large pot to 350°F (180°C).
5. Dip the prepared vegetables into the tempura batter, coating them evenly.
6. Carefully place the battered vegetables into the hot oil, a few pieces at a time, making sure not to overcrowd the fryer.
7. Fry the vegetables for 2-3 minutes, or until they are golden brown and crispy.
8. Use a slotted spoon or tongs to remove the fried vegetables from the oil and transfer them to a plate lined with paper towels to drain excess oil.
9. Sprinkle the tempura vegetables with salt while they are still hot.
10. Repeat the battering and frying process with the remaining vegetables.
11. Serve the tempura vegetables hot, with your choice of dipping sauce on the side.

Enjoy your crispy and delicious homemade tempura vegetables as a snack or appetizer!

Miso Soup

Ingredients:

- 4 cups dashi (Japanese soup stock) or vegetable broth
- 3 tablespoons miso paste (white or red miso)
- 1 block (about 8 ounces) silken tofu, cut into small cubes
- 2 green onions, thinly sliced
- 1 sheet nori (seaweed), cut into thin strips (optional)
- 1 tablespoon soy sauce (optional)
- 1 teaspoon sesame oil (optional)

Instructions:

1. In a medium pot, bring the dashi or vegetable broth to a gentle simmer over medium heat.
2. In a small bowl, dilute the miso paste with a few tablespoons of the hot broth to make it easier to incorporate.
3. Add the diluted miso paste to the pot of simmering broth, stirring well to dissolve the miso.
4. Add the cubed tofu to the soup and let it simmer gently for about 2-3 minutes.
5. Taste the soup and adjust the flavor with soy sauce if desired.
6. Remove the pot from the heat and add the sliced green onions.
7. If using, drizzle sesame oil over the soup for added flavor.
8. Ladle the miso soup into bowls and garnish with nori strips, if desired.
9. Serve the miso soup hot as a comforting and nourishing appetizer or side dish.

Enjoy your homemade miso soup! Feel free to customize it by adding other ingredients such as mushrooms, spinach, or wakame seaweed according to your preference.

Yakitori Skewers

Ingredients:

- 1 lb (450g) boneless, skinless chicken thighs, cut into bite-sized pieces
- 1/4 cup soy sauce
- 1/4 cup mirin (Japanese sweet rice wine)
- 2 tablespoons sake (Japanese rice wine) or dry white wine
- 2 tablespoons brown sugar
- 2 cloves garlic, minced
- 1 teaspoon grated ginger
- Bamboo skewers, soaked in water for at least 30 minutes

Instructions:

1. In a bowl, combine the soy sauce, mirin, sake, brown sugar, minced garlic, and grated ginger to make the yakitori marinade.
2. Thread the chicken thigh pieces onto the soaked bamboo skewers, dividing them evenly among the skewers.
3. Place the skewers in a shallow dish or resealable plastic bag, and pour the marinade over them, ensuring the chicken is well coated. Reserve a small amount of marinade for basting.
4. Marinate the chicken skewers in the refrigerator for at least 30 minutes, or up to 2 hours, turning occasionally to ensure even marination.
5. Preheat your grill or broiler to medium-high heat.
6. Remove the chicken skewers from the marinade and discard the excess marinade.
7. Grill or broil the chicken skewers for 4-5 minutes on each side, or until the chicken is cooked through and nicely charred on the outside. Baste the skewers with the reserved marinade while grilling.
8. Once the chicken is cooked, transfer the skewers to a serving platter.
9. Serve the yakitori skewers hot, garnished with sliced green onions and sesame seeds if desired.
10. Enjoy your delicious homemade yakitori skewers as a tasty appetizer or main dish!

Feel free to customize your yakitori skewers by adding vegetables such as bell peppers, onions, or mushrooms between the chicken pieces on the skewers.

Tonkatsu Pork Cutlets

Ingredients:

- 4 boneless pork loin chops, about 1/2 inch thick
- Salt and pepper, to taste
- 1/2 cup all-purpose flour
- 2 large eggs, beaten
- 1 cup panko breadcrumbs
- Vegetable oil, for frying
- Tonkatsu sauce (store-bought or homemade), for serving
- Shredded cabbage, for serving
- Cooked rice, for serving

Instructions:

1. Place each pork chop between two sheets of plastic wrap or wax paper. Use a meat mallet or rolling pin to pound the pork chops until they are about 1/4 inch thick. Season both sides of the pork chops with salt and pepper.
2. Set up a breading station with three shallow dishes. Place the flour in one dish, the beaten eggs in another dish, and the panko breadcrumbs in the third dish.
3. Dredge each pork chop in the flour, shaking off any excess.
4. Dip the floured pork chops into the beaten eggs, allowing any excess to drip off.
5. Coat the pork chops in the panko breadcrumbs, pressing gently to adhere the breadcrumbs to the meat.
6. Heat vegetable oil in a large skillet or frying pan over medium heat until it reaches about 350°F (180°C).
7. Carefully add the breaded pork chops to the hot oil, working in batches if necessary to avoid overcrowding the pan. Fry the pork chops for 3-4 minutes on each side, or until they are golden brown and crispy.
8. Once the pork chops are cooked through and crispy, transfer them to a plate lined with paper towels to drain excess oil.
9. Serve the tonkatsu pork cutlets hot, accompanied by tonkatsu sauce for dipping, shredded cabbage, and cooked rice on the side.
10. Enjoy your delicious homemade tonkatsu pork cutlets as a comforting and satisfying meal!

Feel free to garnish your tonkatsu pork cutlets with a sprinkle of sesame seeds and serve with lemon wedges for extra flavor.

Okonomiyaki Pancakes

Ingredients:

- 2 cups shredded cabbage
- 1/2 cup all-purpose flour
- 1/4 cup water
- 2 large eggs
- 2 green onions, thinly sliced
- 1/2 cup cooked shrimp, chopped (optional)
- 1/2 cup cooked pork belly or bacon, chopped (optional)
- 1/4 cup pickled ginger, chopped (optional)
- Vegetable oil, for frying
- Okonomiyaki sauce (store-bought or homemade), for serving
- Japanese mayonnaise, for serving
- Bonito flakes (katsuobushi), for garnish (optional)
- Aonori (dried green seaweed flakes), for garnish (optional)

Instructions:

1. In a large mixing bowl, combine the shredded cabbage, flour, water, and eggs. Mix until well combined and the cabbage is evenly coated with the batter.
2. Add the sliced green onions and any optional ingredients such as cooked shrimp, pork belly or bacon, and pickled ginger to the batter. Stir to distribute the ingredients evenly.
3. Heat a little vegetable oil in a large non-stick skillet or griddle over medium heat.
4. Scoop about 1/2 cup of the cabbage mixture onto the skillet, using a spatula to shape it into a round pancake about 1/2 inch thick.
5. Cook the okonomiyaki pancake for 4-5 minutes on each side, or until golden brown and crispy.
6. Repeat with the remaining batter, adding more oil to the skillet as needed.
7. Once all the pancakes are cooked, transfer them to serving plates.
8. Drizzle okonomiyaki sauce and Japanese mayonnaise over the pancakes.
9. Sprinkle bonito flakes and aonori over the top for added flavor and garnish, if desired.
10. Serve the okonomiyaki pancakes hot, and enjoy!

Feel free to customize your okonomiyaki pancakes with additional toppings such as sliced cooked squid, octopus, or cheese according to your preference.

Gyoza Dumplings

Ingredients:

- 1 lb (450g) ground pork or chicken
- 2 cups shredded cabbage
- 2 green onions, finely chopped
- 2 cloves garlic, minced
- 1 tablespoon grated ginger
- 2 tablespoons soy sauce
- 1 tablespoon sesame oil
- 1 teaspoon sugar
- 1/2 teaspoon salt
- 1/4 teaspoon black pepper
- 1 package round gyoza wrappers (about 30 wrappers)
- Vegetable oil, for frying

For dipping sauce:

- 1/4 cup soy sauce
- 2 tablespoons rice vinegar
- 1 teaspoon sesame oil
- 1 teaspoon chili oil (optional)
- 1 teaspoon finely chopped green onions (optional)

Instructions:

1. In a large mixing bowl, combine the ground pork or chicken, shredded cabbage, chopped green onions, minced garlic, grated ginger, soy sauce, sesame oil, sugar, salt, and black pepper. Mix well until all ingredients are evenly incorporated.
2. To assemble the gyoza dumplings, place a small spoonful of the filling in the center of a gyoza wrapper. Wet the edges of the wrapper with water using your finger.
3. Fold the wrapper in half over the filling to create a half-moon shape, then pinch and pleat the edges together to seal. Repeat with the remaining wrappers and filling.
4. Heat a small amount of vegetable oil in a large non-stick skillet or frying pan over medium heat.

5. Place the gyoza dumplings in the skillet in a single layer, making sure they are not touching each other.
6. Cook the dumplings for 2-3 minutes, or until the bottoms are golden brown.
7. Carefully pour about 1/4 cup of water into the skillet and immediately cover with a lid. Steam the dumplings for 6-8 minutes, or until the filling is cooked through and the wrappers are translucent.
8. Remove the lid and let any excess water evaporate. Continue cooking the dumplings uncovered for another minute or until the bottoms are crisp again.
9. While the gyoza dumplings are cooking, prepare the dipping sauce by combining soy sauce, rice vinegar, sesame oil, and chili oil in a small bowl. Garnish with finely chopped green onions if desired.
10. Serve the gyoza dumplings hot, with the dipping sauce on the side.
11. Enjoy your delicious homemade gyoza dumplings as an appetizer or main dish!

Feel free to customize your gyoza dumplings by adding other ingredients such as chopped shrimp, mushrooms, or tofu to the filling according to your preference.

Katsu Curry

Ingredients:

For the Curry Sauce:

- 2 tablespoons vegetable oil
- 1 onion, finely chopped
- 2 carrots, diced
- 2 potatoes, diced
- 2 cloves garlic, minced
- 2 tablespoons curry powder
- 1 tablespoon flour
- 2 cups vegetable or chicken broth
- 2 tablespoons soy sauce
- 1 tablespoon honey or sugar
- Salt and pepper, to taste

For the Breaded Cutlets (Tonkatsu):

- 4 boneless pork loin chops or chicken breasts, pounded to about 1/2-inch thickness
- Salt and pepper, to taste
- 1/2 cup all-purpose flour
- 2 large eggs, beaten
- 1 cup panko breadcrumbs
- Vegetable oil, for frying

For Serving:

- Cooked rice
- Chopped green onions, for garnish (optional)

Instructions:

1. Heat vegetable oil in a large skillet over medium heat. Add the chopped onion, diced carrots, and potatoes. Cook until the vegetables are softened, about 5-7 minutes.
2. Add the minced garlic and curry powder to the skillet. Cook for another 2 minutes, stirring constantly, until fragrant.
3. Sprinkle the flour over the vegetables and stir to coat. Cook for 1-2 minutes to cook off the raw flour taste.
4. Gradually pour in the vegetable or chicken broth, stirring constantly to prevent lumps from forming. Bring the mixture to a simmer.
5. Stir in the soy sauce and honey or sugar. Season with salt and pepper to taste. Simmer the curry sauce for 15-20 minutes, or until thickened.
6. While the curry sauce is simmering, prepare the breaded cutlets (Tonkatsu). Season the pork or chicken with salt and pepper.
7. Set up a breading station with three shallow dishes: one with flour, one with beaten eggs, and one with panko breadcrumbs.
8. Dredge each pork or chicken cutlet in flour, shaking off any excess. Dip into the beaten eggs, then coat evenly with panko breadcrumbs, pressing gently to adhere.
9. Heat vegetable oil in a large skillet or frying pan over medium-high heat. Fry the breaded cutlets for 4-5 minutes on each side, or until golden brown and cooked through. Transfer to a plate lined with paper towels to drain excess oil.
10. Once the curry sauce is thickened and the breaded cutlets are cooked, serve the Katsu Curry by slicing the cutlets and arranging them over cooked rice. Ladle the curry sauce over the top. Garnish with chopped green onions if desired.
11. Enjoy your delicious homemade Katsu Curry!

Chirashi Sushi Bowl

Ingredients:

For the Sushi Rice:

- 2 cups sushi rice
- 2 cups water
- 1/4 cup rice vinegar
- 2 tablespoons sugar
- 1 teaspoon salt

For the Toppings:

- Assorted sashimi (such as tuna, salmon, yellowtail, or shrimp), thinly sliced
- Sliced cucumber
- Sliced avocado
- Shredded nori seaweed
- Pickled ginger (gari)
- Wasabi paste
- Soy sauce

Optional Garnishes:

- Thinly sliced green onions
- Toasted sesame seeds
- Tobiko (flying fish roe)

Instructions:

1. Rinse the sushi rice under cold water until the water runs clear. Drain well.
2. In a rice cooker or medium saucepan, combine the rinsed rice and water. Cook according to the rice cooker's instructions or bring to a boil, then reduce heat to low, cover, and simmer for about 15-20 minutes, or until the rice is cooked and tender.
3. In a small saucepan, heat the rice vinegar, sugar, and salt over low heat, stirring until the sugar and salt are dissolved. Remove from heat and let cool.
4. Once the rice is cooked, transfer it to a large bowl and gently fold in the seasoned vinegar mixture. Be careful not to overmix; you want to keep the grains of rice intact.

5. Allow the sushi rice to cool to room temperature while you prepare the toppings.
6. Arrange the sliced sashimi, cucumber, avocado, and any other desired toppings on top of the sushi rice in individual serving bowls or a large serving platter.
7. Garnish the Chirashi Sushi Bowl with shredded nori seaweed, pickled ginger, and wasabi paste.
8. Serve the Chirashi Sushi Bowl with soy sauce on the side for dipping.
9. Optionally, garnish with thinly sliced green onions, toasted sesame seeds, and tobiko (flying fish roe) for added flavor and texture.
10. Enjoy your homemade Chirashi Sushi Bowl as a colorful and delicious meal!

Udon Noodle Stir-Fry

Ingredients:

- 8 ounces (about 225g) udon noodles
- 2 tablespoons vegetable oil
- 2 cloves garlic, minced
- 1 small onion, thinly sliced
- 1 bell pepper, thinly sliced
- 1 carrot, julienned or thinly sliced
- 1 cup sliced mushrooms (such as shiitake, cremini, or button mushrooms)
- 2 cups baby spinach or chopped kale
- 1/4 cup soy sauce
- 2 tablespoons oyster sauce (optional)
- 1 tablespoon mirin (Japanese sweet rice wine) or rice vinegar
- 1 teaspoon sesame oil
- 1 tablespoon sesame seeds, for garnish (optional)
- Thinly sliced green onions, for garnish (optional)

Instructions:

1. Cook the udon noodles according to the package instructions. Drain and rinse under cold water to prevent sticking. Set aside.
2. In a large skillet or wok, heat the vegetable oil over medium-high heat.
3. Add the minced garlic and sliced onion to the skillet. Stir-fry for 1-2 minutes, or until the onion is translucent and fragrant.
4. Add the sliced bell pepper, julienned carrot, and sliced mushrooms to the skillet. Stir-fry for 3-4 minutes, or until the vegetables are tender-crisp.
5. Add the cooked udon noodles and baby spinach or chopped kale to the skillet. Stir-fry for another 2-3 minutes, or until the noodles are heated through and the spinach or kale is wilted.
6. In a small bowl, whisk together the soy sauce, oyster sauce (if using), mirin or rice vinegar, and sesame oil.
7. Pour the sauce mixture over the udon noodle stir-fry in the skillet. Toss everything together until well coated in the sauce.
8. Cook for an additional minute, allowing the flavors to meld together.
9. Remove the skillet from the heat and transfer the udon noodle stir-fry to serving plates or bowls.

10. Garnish with sesame seeds and thinly sliced green onions, if desired.
11. Serve the udon noodle stir-fry hot, and enjoy!

Feel free to customize your udon noodle stir-fry by adding other vegetables or protein such as tofu, chicken, shrimp, or beef according to your preference. Adjust the seasonings to taste, and enjoy a delicious and satisfying meal!

Soba Noodle Salad

Ingredients:

For the Salad:

- 8 ounces (about 225g) soba noodles
- 2 cups shredded cabbage or coleslaw mix
- 1 large carrot, julienned or grated
- 1 cucumber, julienned or thinly sliced
- 1 bell pepper, thinly sliced
- 2 green onions, thinly sliced
- 1/4 cup chopped fresh cilantro or parsley (optional)
- 1/4 cup chopped roasted peanuts or cashews (optional)
- Toasted sesame seeds, for garnish (optional)

For the Dressing:

- 1/4 cup soy sauce
- 2 tablespoons rice vinegar
- 1 tablespoon sesame oil
- 1 tablespoon honey or maple syrup
- 1 teaspoon grated ginger
- 1 clove garlic, minced
- Red pepper flakes, to taste (optional)

Instructions:

1. Cook the soba noodles according to the package instructions. Drain and rinse under cold water to stop the cooking process and prevent sticking. Set aside to cool.
2. In a large mixing bowl, combine the shredded cabbage, julienned carrot, sliced cucumber, sliced bell pepper, sliced green onions, and chopped cilantro or parsley (if using).
3. Add the cooled soba noodles to the bowl with the vegetables.

4. In a small bowl, whisk together the soy sauce, rice vinegar, sesame oil, honey or maple syrup, grated ginger, minced garlic, and red pepper flakes (if using) to make the dressing.
5. Pour the dressing over the soba noodle salad and toss until everything is well coated in the dressing.
6. Taste and adjust the seasoning as needed, adding more soy sauce, rice vinegar, honey, or red pepper flakes according to your preference.
7. Transfer the soba noodle salad to a serving platter or individual plates.
8. Garnish with chopped roasted peanuts or cashews and toasted sesame seeds, if desired.
9. Serve the soba noodle salad immediately, or refrigerate for 30 minutes to allow the flavors to meld together before serving.
10. Enjoy your refreshing and flavorful homemade soba noodle salad as a light and nutritious meal!

Oyakodon Chicken and Egg Rice Bowl

Ingredients:

- 2 boneless, skinless chicken thighs, thinly sliced
- 1 onion, thinly sliced
- 3 large eggs
- 1 cup dashi (Japanese soup stock)
- 3 tablespoons soy sauce
- 2 tablespoons mirin (Japanese sweet rice wine)
- 1 tablespoon sugar
- 2 cups cooked Japanese short-grain rice
- Sliced green onions, for garnish
- Nori seaweed, cut into thin strips, for garnish (optional)

Instructions:

1. In a medium-sized skillet or pan, combine the dashi, soy sauce, mirin, and sugar. Bring the mixture to a gentle simmer over medium heat.
2. Add the thinly sliced onions to the simmering liquid and cook until they become translucent, about 2-3 minutes.
3. Add the thinly sliced chicken thighs to the skillet and cook until they are no longer pink, about 3-4 minutes.
4. In a separate bowl, beat the eggs lightly.
5. Once the chicken is cooked through, pour the beaten eggs evenly over the chicken and onions in the skillet. Allow the eggs to cook undisturbed until they are mostly set, but still slightly runny on top.
6. To assemble the Oyakodon bowls, divide the cooked rice among serving bowls.
7. Carefully spoon the chicken, onions, and partially cooked eggs over the rice in each bowl.
8. Return the skillet to low heat and cover with a lid for another minute to finish cooking the eggs to your desired consistency.
9. Garnish the Oyakodon bowls with sliced green onions and nori seaweed strips (if using).
10. Serve the Oyakodon bowls hot, and enjoy this delicious and comforting Japanese meal!

Feel free to adjust the seasoning of the sauce according to your taste preferences. Oyakodon is typically served with a side of pickled ginger and a bowl of miso soup for a complete meal.

Takoyaki Octopus Balls

Ingredients:

For the Batter:

- 1 1/2 cups all-purpose flour
- 2 cups dashi (Japanese soup stock) or water
- 2 large eggs
- 1 tablespoon soy sauce
- 1 tablespoon mirin (Japanese sweet rice wine)
- 1/2 teaspoon salt

For the Filling:

- 1/2 cup cooked octopus, chopped into small pieces
- 1/4 cup chopped pickled ginger (beni shoga)
- 2 green onions, thinly sliced

For Cooking and Serving:

- Takoyaki sauce (store-bought or homemade)
- Japanese mayonnaise
- Aonori (dried green seaweed flakes)
- Katsuobushi (bonito flakes)

Special Equipment:

- Takoyaki pan (a special pan with round molds)

Instructions:

1. In a large mixing bowl, whisk together the all-purpose flour, dashi or water, eggs, soy sauce, mirin, and salt until smooth. The batter should be similar in consistency to pancake batter. Let the batter rest for about 30 minutes.
2. Heat the takoyaki pan over medium heat. Grease the molds generously with oil using a brush or paper towel.
3. Once the pan is hot, pour the batter into each mold, filling them about halfway full.

4. Place a piece of chopped octopus, some chopped pickled ginger, and a few slices of green onion into each mold.
5. Once the edges of the takoyaki start to cook and set, use a skewer or chopsticks to start rotating each ball so that the uncooked batter flows into the bottom of the mold and forms a ball shape. Keep rotating until the balls are evenly cooked and golden brown on all sides, about 6-8 minutes.
6. Transfer the cooked takoyaki to a plate.
7. Drizzle takoyaki sauce and Japanese mayonnaise over the top of the takoyaki.
8. Sprinkle with aonori and katsuobushi.
9. Serve the takoyaki hot, and enjoy!

Takoyaki is typically enjoyed as a snack or appetizer. Be careful when eating as the filling may be hot.

Sashimi Platter

Ingredients:

Assorted sashimi-grade fish (such as tuna, salmon, yellowtail, snapper, mackerel, or squid), thinly sliced
Pickled ginger (gari)
Wasabi paste
Soy sauce
Optional garnishes:
Thinly sliced cucumber
Avocado slices
Radish sprouts (kaiware)
Shiso leaves

Edible flowers

Instructions:

1. Start by selecting a variety of fresh sashimi-grade fish from your local fish market or reputable seafood supplier. Make sure the fish is properly cleaned and sliced thinly.
2. Prepare a platter or large serving dish to arrange the sashimi. You can use a traditional wooden sushi board, a ceramic plate, or a decorative serving tray.
3. Arrange the sliced fish on the platter in an attractive manner. You can arrange them in rows, fan them out in a circular pattern, or layer them on top of each other to create height.
4. Place small piles of pickled ginger (gari) and wasabi paste in between the fish slices for seasoning.
5. Serve soy sauce in small dipping bowls or pour it into a small pitcher for guests to drizzle over their sashimi.
6. If using optional garnishes, arrange them decoratively around the sashimi on the platter. Thinly sliced cucumber can be rolled or folded into decorative shapes, avocado slices can be fanned out, and radish sprouts or shiso leaves can be scattered around for color and texture.
7. For an extra touch of elegance, you can garnish the platter with edible flowers or decorative elements such as bamboo leaves.
8. Serve the sashimi platter immediately to enjoy the freshness of the fish.

9. Encourage guests to customize their sashimi experience by trying different combinations of fish, garnishes, and seasonings.
10. Enjoy your stunning sashimi platter as a delicious and visually appealing appetizer or main course!

Karaage Fried Chicken

Ingredients:

- 1 lb (about 450g) boneless, skinless chicken thighs, cut into bite-sized pieces
- 3 tablespoons soy sauce
- 2 tablespoons sake (Japanese rice wine) or dry sherry
- 1 tablespoon grated ginger
- 2 cloves garlic, minced
- 1 tablespoon sesame oil
- 1 tablespoon sugar
- 1/2 cup potato starch or cornstarch
- Vegetable oil, for frying
- Lemon wedges, for serving
- Shredded cabbage, for serving (optional)
- Japanese mayonnaise, for dipping (optional)
- Shichimi togarashi (Japanese seven spice), for sprinkling (optional)

Instructions:

1. In a bowl, combine the soy sauce, sake, grated ginger, minced garlic, sesame oil, and sugar. Stir until the sugar is dissolved.
2. Add the chicken pieces to the marinade and toss until they are well coated. Cover the bowl and refrigerate for at least 30 minutes, or up to 4 hours, to allow the flavors to meld.
3. Heat vegetable oil in a large skillet or deep fryer to 350°F (180°C).
4. Place the potato starch or cornstarch in a shallow dish. Remove the chicken from the marinade and dredge each piece in the starch, shaking off any excess.
5. Carefully add the coated chicken pieces to the hot oil in batches, making sure not to overcrowd the skillet. Fry the chicken for 5-7 minutes, or until golden brown and cooked through, turning occasionally for even cooking.
6. Use a slotted spoon or wire mesh strainer to transfer the fried chicken to a plate lined with paper towels to drain excess oil.
7. Repeat the frying process with the remaining chicken pieces.
8. Serve the Karaage hot, with lemon wedges on the side for squeezing over the chicken.

9. Optionally, serve shredded cabbage on the side as a refreshing accompaniment. You can also offer Japanese mayonnaise for dipping and sprinkle Shichimi togarashi for extra flavor and spice.
10. Enjoy your delicious homemade Karaage as a snack, appetizer, or main course!

Karaage is best enjoyed fresh and hot, but leftovers can be stored in an airtight container in the refrigerator for up to 2 days. Simply reheat in the oven or toaster oven to restore crispiness before serving.

Japanese Curry Rice

Ingredients:

- 1 lb (about 450g) protein of your choice (chicken, beef, pork, tofu), cut into bite-sized pieces
- 2 onions, thinly sliced
- 2 carrots, peeled and diced
- 2 potatoes, peeled and diced
- 2 cloves garlic, minced
- 2 tablespoons vegetable oil
- 4 cups water or chicken/beef broth
- 1 box (200g) Japanese curry roux (available in mild, medium, or hot)
- Cooked Japanese short-grain rice, for serving

Optional garnishes:

- Fukujinzuke (Japanese pickled vegetables)
- Beni shoga (pickled ginger)
- Pickled radish
- Thinly sliced green onions

Instructions:

1. Heat vegetable oil in a large pot over medium heat. Add the minced garlic and sliced onions. Sauté until the onions are softened and translucent, about 5 minutes.
2. Add the diced carrots and potatoes to the pot. Cook for another 5 minutes, stirring occasionally.
3. Push the vegetables to one side of the pot and add the bite-sized pieces of protein to the other side. Cook until the meat is browned on all sides.
4. Pour in the water or broth, ensuring that the meat and vegetables are fully submerged. Bring the liquid to a boil, then reduce the heat and let it simmer uncovered for about 15-20 minutes, or until the vegetables are tender and the meat is cooked through.
5. Break the Japanese curry roux into pieces and add them to the pot. Stir until the roux is completely dissolved into the liquid and the curry thickens, about 5 minutes.

6. Taste the curry and adjust the seasoning if necessary. If you prefer a thicker curry, you can simmer it for a few more minutes to reduce the liquid.
7. Serve the Japanese Curry Rice hot over cooked Japanese short-grain rice.
8. Garnish with fukujinzuke, beni shoga, pickled radish, or thinly sliced green onions, if desired.
9. Enjoy your homemade Japanese Curry Rice as a comforting and satisfying meal!

Japanese Curry Rice is a versatile dish, and you can customize it by adding other vegetables such as peas, bell peppers, or mushrooms according to your preference.

Adjust the spiciness level by choosing mild, medium, or hot curry roux.

Yaki Udon Stir-Fry

Ingredients:

- 8 ounces (about 225g) udon noodles
- 2 tablespoons vegetable oil
- 2 cloves garlic, minced
- 1 onion, thinly sliced
- 1 carrot, julienned
- 1 bell pepper, thinly sliced
- 1 cup sliced mushrooms (such as shiitake, cremini, or button mushrooms)
- 2 cups shredded cabbage or coleslaw mix
- 1/4 cup soy sauce
- 2 tablespoons oyster sauce
- 1 tablespoon mirin (Japanese sweet rice wine) or rice vinegar
- 1 teaspoon sesame oil
- Salt and pepper, to taste
- Thinly sliced green onions, for garnish
- Toasted sesame seeds, for garnish

Instructions:

1. Cook the udon noodles according to the package instructions. Drain and rinse under cold water to prevent sticking. Set aside.
2. In a large skillet or wok, heat the vegetable oil over medium-high heat.
3. Add the minced garlic and thinly sliced onion to the skillet. Sauté for 1-2 minutes, or until the onion is softened and fragrant.
4. Add the julienned carrot, thinly sliced bell pepper, and sliced mushrooms to the skillet. Stir-fry for 3-4 minutes, or until the vegetables are tender-crisp.
5. Add the shredded cabbage or coleslaw mix to the skillet. Stir-fry for another 2-3 minutes, or until the cabbage is wilted.
6. Add the cooked udon noodles to the skillet, along with the soy sauce, oyster sauce, mirin or rice vinegar, and sesame oil. Toss everything together until well combined.
7. Cook for an additional 2-3 minutes, stirring frequently, to heat the noodles through and allow the flavors to meld together.
8. Taste the yaki udon stir-fry and adjust the seasoning with salt and pepper if needed.

9. Transfer the yaki udon stir-fry to serving plates or bowls.
10. Garnish with thinly sliced green onions and toasted sesame seeds.
11. Serve the yaki udon stir-fry hot, and enjoy!

Yaki Udon Stir-Fry is a versatile dish, and you can customize it by adding other ingredients such as tofu, shrimp, chicken, or beef according to your preference. Feel free to adjust the seasonings and garnishes to suit your taste, and enjoy this delicious and satisfying Japanese-inspired stir-fry!

Oden Hot Pot

Ingredients:

- Assorted ingredients for Oden (examples include daikon radish, konnyaku, boiled eggs, fish cakes, tofu, mushrooms, and cabbage)
- 6 cups dashi (Japanese soup stock)
- 1/4 cup soy sauce
- 2 tablespoons mirin (Japanese sweet rice wine)
- 1 tablespoon sugar
- 1 teaspoon salt
- Mustard or karashi (Japanese hot mustard), for serving (optional)

Instructions:

1. Prepare the ingredients for Oden by cutting them into bite-sized pieces or slices. Common ingredients include daikon radish cut into thick rounds, konnyaku sliced into rectangles, boiled eggs peeled and halved, fish cakes sliced, tofu cut into cubes, mushrooms sliced, and cabbage cut into wedges.
2. In a large pot, combine the dashi, soy sauce, mirin, sugar, and salt. Bring the mixture to a simmer over medium heat.
3. Add the prepared ingredients to the pot of simmering broth. Start with the ingredients that require the longest cooking time, such as daikon radish and konnyaku. Then add the rest of the ingredients, arranging them in the pot.
4. Cover the pot with a lid and let the Oden simmer gently over low heat for about 30-45 minutes, or until all the ingredients are tender and infused with flavor.
5. Taste the broth and adjust the seasoning with more soy sauce, mirin, sugar, or salt if needed.
6. Once the ingredients are cooked through and the flavors have melded together, the Oden is ready to serve.
7. Ladle the Oden into serving bowls, making sure to distribute a variety of ingredients in each bowl.
8. Serve the Oden hot, with mustard or karashi on the side for dipping if desired.
9. Enjoy your comforting and flavorful Oden hot pot as a delicious and satisfying meal!

Oden is often enjoyed during colder months in Japan and is a popular dish for gatherings with family and friends. Feel free to customize your Oden with your favorite ingredients and adjust the seasoning to suit your taste preferences.

Nikujaga Beef and Potato Stew

Ingredients:

- 1 lb (about 450g) thinly sliced beef (such as beef chuck or sirloin)
- 2 potatoes, peeled and cut into chunks
- 1 onion, thinly sliced
- 2 carrots, peeled and cut into chunks
- 1 cup shirataki noodles (optional)
- 2 cups dashi (Japanese soup stock)
- 1/4 cup soy sauce
- 2 tablespoons mirin (Japanese sweet rice wine)
- 1 tablespoon sugar
- 1 tablespoon vegetable oil
- Salt and pepper, to taste
- Thinly sliced green onions, for garnish (optional)

Instructions:

1. Heat vegetable oil in a large pot over medium heat. Add the thinly sliced beef and cook until browned on all sides.
2. Add the sliced onion to the pot and sauté until softened and translucent.
3. Add the chunks of potatoes and carrots to the pot, along with the shirataki noodles if using.
4. Pour the dashi (Japanese soup stock) over the ingredients in the pot. Bring the liquid to a simmer.
5. Add the soy sauce, mirin, and sugar to the pot. Stir to combine.
6. Cover the pot with a lid and let the Nikujaga simmer gently over low heat for about 20-30 minutes, or until the potatoes and carrots are tender.
7. Taste the Nikujaga and adjust the seasoning with salt and pepper if needed.
8. Once the vegetables are cooked through and the flavors have melded together, the Nikujaga is ready to serve.
9. Ladle the Nikujaga into serving bowls, making sure to include a generous portion of beef, potatoes, carrots, and shirataki noodles in each bowl.
10. Garnish the Nikujaga with thinly sliced green onions if desired.
11. Serve the Nikujaga hot, and enjoy your comforting and flavorful beef and potato stew!

Nikujaga is often enjoyed as a hearty and comforting meal, especially during colder months in Japan. Feel free to customize your Nikujaga by adding other vegetables such as mushrooms, green beans, or peas according to your preference. Adjust the seasoning to suit your taste, and enjoy this delicious and satisfying Japanese stew!

Sukiyaki Beef Hot Pot

Ingredients:

- 1 lb (about 450g) thinly sliced beef (such as beef sirloin or ribeye)
- 1/2 cup soy sauce
- 1/4 cup mirin (Japanese sweet rice wine)
- 1/4 cup sugar
- 1 cup dashi (Japanese soup stock)
- 1 onion, thinly sliced
- 2 green onions, cut into 2-inch lengths
- 1/2 block (about 7 oz or 200g) firm tofu, cut into cubes
- 1/2 bunch of shungiku (chrysanthemum greens) or spinach, trimmed and cut into bite-sized pieces
- 1 package (about 7 oz or 200g) shirataki noodles, rinsed and drained
- 6-8 shiitake mushrooms, stems removed and caps sliced
- 1/2 head of napa cabbage, sliced
- 4 eggs (optional)
- Cooked Japanese short-grain rice, for serving

Instructions:

1. In a small bowl, mix together the soy sauce, mirin, sugar, and dashi to make the Sukiyaki sauce. Set aside.
2. Heat a large skillet or a sukiyaki pan over medium heat. Add a small amount of vegetable oil if needed.
3. Add the thinly sliced beef to the skillet and cook until lightly browned.
4. Pour the Sukiyaki sauce over the beef in the skillet. Add the sliced onion, green onions, tofu cubes, shungiku or spinach, shirataki noodles, shiitake mushrooms, and napa cabbage to the skillet.
5. Let the ingredients simmer in the Sukiyaki sauce until the vegetables are tender and the beef is cooked through, about 5-7 minutes.
6. If using eggs, crack them into individual small bowls or cups.
7. Once the Sukiyaki is ready to serve, crack the eggs into the skillet or individual serving bowls. Allow the eggs to cook slightly in the hot Sukiyaki broth.
8. Serve the Sukiyaki hot with cooked Japanese short-grain rice on the side.
9. To eat, dip the cooked Sukiyaki ingredients and rice into the raw egg before eating.

10. Enjoy your delicious and comforting Sukiyaki hot pot!

Sukiyaki is a popular dish in Japan, especially during the colder months. Feel free to adjust the ingredients according to your preference, and enjoy this flavorful and hearty Japanese hot pot with family and friends!

Onigiri Rice Balls

Ingredients:

- 2 cups Japanese short-grain rice (such as sushi rice)
- 2 1/2 cups water
- 1/4 cup rice vinegar
- 2 tablespoons sugar
- 1 teaspoon salt
- Filling options (such as umeboshi (pickled plum), tuna salad, cooked salmon, grilled chicken, cooked vegetables, or furikake seasoning)
- Nori seaweed sheets, cut into strips (optional, for wrapping)

Instructions:

1. Rinse the rice under cold water until the water runs clear. Drain well.
2. In a rice cooker or medium saucepan, combine the rinsed rice and water. Cook according to the rice cooker's instructions or bring to a boil, then reduce heat to low, cover, and simmer for about 15-20 minutes, or until the rice is cooked and tender.
3. In a small saucepan, heat the rice vinegar, sugar, and salt over low heat, stirring until the sugar and salt are dissolved. Remove from heat and let cool.
4. Once the rice is cooked, transfer it to a large bowl and gently fold in the seasoned vinegar mixture. Be careful not to overmix; you want to keep the grains of rice intact.
5. Allow the seasoned rice to cool to room temperature while you prepare the fillings.
6. To assemble the onigiri, wet your hands with water to prevent the rice from sticking. Take a small handful of seasoned rice and flatten it slightly in the palm of your hand.
7. Place a small amount of your desired filling in the center of the rice.
8. Gently fold the rice around the filling, shaping it into a triangle, ball, or cylindrical shape. Press firmly to compact the rice and filling together.
9. If using nori seaweed, wrap a strip of nori around the onigiri to secure it and provide extra flavor.
10. Repeat the process with the remaining rice and fillings.
11. Serve the onigiri at room temperature or slightly warm.

Onigiri is a versatile dish, and you can customize it with your favorite fillings. It's perfect for a quick snack, a packed lunch, or a picnic. Enjoy your homemade onigiri rice balls!

Tofu Teriyaki

Ingredients:

- 1 block (about 14 oz or 400g) firm tofu, drained and pressed
- 2 tablespoons soy sauce
- 2 tablespoons mirin (Japanese sweet rice wine)
- 1 tablespoon sake (Japanese rice wine) or dry sherry
- 1 tablespoon sugar
- 1 tablespoon vegetable oil, for frying
- Sesame seeds, for garnish (optional)
- Thinly sliced green onions, for garnish (optional)

Instructions:

1. Cut the block of tofu into slices or cubes, depending on your preference. Pat the tofu dry with paper towels to remove excess moisture.
2. In a small bowl, whisk together the soy sauce, mirin, sake, and sugar to make the teriyaki sauce. Set aside.
3. Heat the vegetable oil in a large skillet or non-stick frying pan over medium-high heat.
4. Add the tofu slices or cubes to the skillet in a single layer, making sure not to overcrowd the pan. Fry the tofu until golden brown and crispy on all sides, about 3-4 minutes per side.
5. Once the tofu is browned, reduce the heat to low and pour the teriyaki sauce over the tofu in the skillet.
6. Let the tofu simmer in the teriyaki sauce for 2-3 minutes, or until the sauce has thickened slightly and coats the tofu.
7. Carefully flip the tofu pieces to ensure they are evenly coated in the teriyaki sauce.
8. Once the sauce has thickened to your desired consistency, remove the skillet from the heat.
9. Transfer the tofu teriyaki to a serving platter or individual plates.
10. Garnish with sesame seeds and thinly sliced green onions, if desired.
11. Serve the tofu teriyaki hot, accompanied by steamed rice or your favorite side dishes.

Enjoy your delicious homemade Tofu Teriyaki as a flavorful and satisfying vegetarian dish!

Hiyayakko Cold Tofu

Ingredients:

- 1 block (about 14 oz or 400g) silken tofu
- Soy sauce, for drizzling
- Grated ginger, for garnish
- Thinly sliced green onions, for garnish
- Toasted sesame seeds, for garnish
- Bonito flakes (katsuobushi), for garnish (optional)

Instructions:

1. Carefully remove the tofu from its packaging and drain any excess liquid.
2. Slice the tofu block into serving-sized pieces and arrange them on individual plates or a serving platter.
3. Drizzle soy sauce over the tofu slices, using as much or as little as you like.
4. Garnish the tofu with grated ginger, thinly sliced green onions, toasted sesame seeds, and bonito flakes (if using).
5. Serve the Hiyayakko immediately, and enjoy!

Hiyayakko is typically served as a refreshing appetizer or side dish, especially during hot weather. It's simple to prepare and allows the delicate flavor of the tofu to shine, enhanced by the umami-rich soy sauce and fragrant toppings. Feel free to adjust the garnishes according to your taste preferences, and enjoy this delicious and nutritious Japanese dish!

Tonjiru Pork Miso Soup

Ingredients:

- 4 cups dashi (Japanese soup stock)
- 200g thinly sliced pork belly or pork shoulder
- 1 small onion, thinly sliced
- 1 carrot, peeled and thinly sliced
- 1 potato, peeled and diced
- 1/2 block (about 150g) firm tofu, cut into small cubes
- 2 tablespoons miso paste (white or red miso)
- 2 green onions, thinly sliced
- 1 tablespoon vegetable oil
- Salt, to taste
- Shichimi togarashi (Japanese seven spice), for garnish (optional)

Instructions:

1. Heat the vegetable oil in a large pot over medium heat. Add the thinly sliced pork and cook until lightly browned.
2. Add the sliced onion to the pot and sauté until softened and translucent.
3. Pour the dashi (Japanese soup stock) into the pot and bring it to a simmer.
4. Add the thinly sliced carrot and diced potato to the pot. Let the vegetables simmer until they are tender, about 10-15 minutes.
5. Once the vegetables are cooked, add the cubed tofu to the pot and simmer for another 2-3 minutes.
6. In a small bowl, dilute the miso paste with a small amount of hot broth from the pot, stirring until smooth.
7. Add the diluted miso paste to the pot and stir well to incorporate it into the soup.
8. Taste the Tonjiru and adjust the seasoning with salt if needed.
9. Add thinly sliced green onions to the pot just before serving.
10. Ladle the Tonjiru into serving bowls and garnish with shichimi togarashi (if using).
11. Serve the Tonjiru hot, and enjoy your comforting and flavorful pork miso soup!

Tonjiru is a hearty and nourishing soup that's perfect for cold weather or anytime you're craving a comforting meal. Feel free to customize your Tonjiru by adding other vegetables or ingredients such as mushrooms, daikon radish, or konjac noodles according to your preference.

Ebi Fry Shrimp

Ingredients:

- 12 large shrimp, peeled and deveined, tails intact
- Salt and pepper, to taste
- All-purpose flour, for dredging
- 1-2 eggs, beaten
- Panko breadcrumbs, for coating
- Vegetable oil, for deep-frying
- Lemon wedges, for serving
- Tonkatsu sauce or tartar sauce, for dipping (optional)

Instructions:

1. Pat the peeled and deveined shrimp dry with paper towels. Season them lightly with salt and pepper.
2. Set up a breading station with three shallow dishes: one with all-purpose flour, one with beaten eggs, and one with panko breadcrumbs.
3. Dredge each shrimp in the flour, shaking off any excess.
4. Dip the floured shrimp into the beaten eggs, coating them evenly.
5. Finally, coat the shrimp in the panko breadcrumbs, pressing gently to adhere.
6. Heat vegetable oil in a deep fryer or large pot to 350°F (180°C).
7. Carefully add the breaded shrimp to the hot oil in batches, making sure not to overcrowd the fryer. Fry the shrimp for about 2-3 minutes, or until golden brown and crispy.
8. Use a slotted spoon or wire mesh strainer to transfer the fried shrimp to a plate lined with paper towels to drain excess oil.
9. Repeat the frying process with the remaining shrimp.
10. Serve the Ebi Fry hot, accompanied by lemon wedges for squeezing over the shrimp. You can also serve them with tonkatsu sauce or tartar sauce for dipping, if desired.
11. Enjoy your crispy and delicious homemade Ebi Fry as a tasty appetizer or main dish!

Ebi Fry is a popular Japanese dish that's sure to please seafood lovers. It's crispy on the outside and juicy on the inside, making it a delightful treat for any occasion. Feel free to customize the seasoning and dipping sauce according to your taste preferences.

Chawanmushi Steamed Egg Custard

Ingredients:

- 2 large eggs
- 1 1/2 cups dashi (Japanese soup stock)
- 1 tablespoon soy sauce
- 1 tablespoon mirin (Japanese sweet rice wine)
- 1/2 teaspoon salt
- 1/2 teaspoon sugar
- Assorted fillings (such as cooked shrimp, chicken, fish cake, shiitake mushrooms, ginkgo nuts, bamboo shoots, or green peas)
- Thinly sliced green onions, for garnish
- Mitsuba leaves or cilantro, for garnish (optional)

Instructions:

1. In a mixing bowl, whisk together the eggs, dashi, soy sauce, mirin, salt, and sugar until well combined.
2. Strain the egg mixture through a fine-mesh sieve into a large measuring cup or bowl to remove any lumps.
3. Prepare your Chawanmushi cups or small heatproof bowls by placing your chosen fillings in the bottom of each cup. You can use a combination of fillings according to your preference.
4. Pour the strained egg mixture over the fillings in each cup, filling them almost to the top.
5. Cover each cup with plastic wrap or aluminum foil to prevent steam from entering during steaming.
6. Place the cups in a steamer basket or on a rack set over a pot of simmering water.
7. Steam the Chawanmushi over medium heat for about 15-20 minutes, or until the custard is set and no longer jiggles when gently shaken.
8. Carefully remove the cups from the steamer and let them cool slightly before serving.
9. Garnish the Chawanmushi with thinly sliced green onions and mitsuba leaves or cilantro, if desired.
10. Serve the Chawanmushi hot as an appetizer or side dish, using a spoon to scoop out the creamy custard and flavorful fillings.

Chawanmushi is a delicate and comforting dish that's perfect for showcasing seasonal ingredients. Feel free to experiment with different fillings and garnishes to create your own unique variations of this classic Japanese dish. Enjoy your homemade Chawanmushi!

Zaru Soba Cold Buckwheat Noodles

Ingredients:

- 8 ounces (about 225g) dried soba noodles
- 4 cups water
- Ice cubes
- 1/4 cup soy sauce
- 2 tablespoons mirin (Japanese sweet rice wine)
- 1 tablespoon rice vinegar
- 1 teaspoon sugar
- Thinly sliced green onions, for garnish
- Wasabi paste, for serving (optional)
- Grated daikon radish, for serving (optional)
- Nori seaweed, cut into thin strips, for garnish (optional)
- Toasted sesame seeds, for garnish (optional)

Instructions:

1. Bring 4 cups of water to a boil in a large pot. Add the dried soba noodles to the boiling water and cook according to the package instructions, usually about 5-6 minutes, or until the noodles are tender but still firm to the bite.
2. While the noodles are cooking, prepare a bowl of ice water.
3. Once the noodles are cooked, immediately drain them and transfer them to the bowl of ice water to stop the cooking process and chill the noodles. Let them sit in the ice water for a few minutes until they are completely cold.
4. While the noodles are chilling, prepare the dipping sauce. In a small bowl, mix together the soy sauce, mirin, rice vinegar, and sugar until well combined.
5. Once the noodles are cold, drain them again and arrange them on a serving plate or individual plates.
6. Serve the chilled soba noodles with the dipping sauce on the side in small individual bowls or sauce dishes.
7. Optionally, garnish the soba noodles with thinly sliced green onions, nori seaweed strips, and toasted sesame seeds.
8. Optionally, serve wasabi paste and grated daikon radish on the side for dipping.
9. To eat, take a small amount of noodles with your chopsticks and dip them into the dipping sauce before slurping them up.
10. Enjoy your refreshing and delicious Zaru Soba cold buckwheat noodles!

Zaru Soba is a popular summer dish in Japan, perfect for cooling down on hot days. Feel free to customize your Zaru Soba with additional toppings or garnishes according to your taste preferences.

Nasu Dengaku Miso-glazed Eggplant

Ingredients:

- 2 small Japanese eggplants or 1 large eggplant
- 2 tablespoons white miso paste
- 1 tablespoon mirin (Japanese sweet rice wine)
- 1 tablespoon sugar
- 1 tablespoon sake (Japanese rice wine) or dry sherry
- Vegetable oil, for brushing
- Toasted sesame seeds, for garnish
- Thinly sliced green onions, for garnish

Instructions:

1. Preheat the oven to 400°F (200°C). Alternatively, you can use a grill or broiler for cooking.
2. Cut the eggplants in half lengthwise. Score the flesh of each half with a crosshatch pattern, being careful not to cut through the skin.
3. In a small bowl, mix together the white miso paste, mirin, sugar, and sake until well combined to make the miso glaze.
4. Place the eggplant halves on a baking sheet lined with parchment paper. Brush the cut sides of the eggplant with a thin layer of vegetable oil.
5. Spoon the miso glaze over the cut sides of the eggplant, spreading it evenly with a spoon or brush.
6. Bake the eggplant in the preheated oven for about 20-25 minutes, or until the flesh is tender and the miso glaze is caramelized and golden brown.
7. Alternatively, if using a grill or broiler, place the eggplant halves cut side down on the grill or under the broiler and cook until charred and tender, then flip them over, brush with the miso glaze, and cook for a few more minutes until caramelized.
8. Once cooked, remove the eggplant from the oven or grill and transfer them to a serving plate.
9. Garnish the Nasu Dengaku with toasted sesame seeds and thinly sliced green onions.
10. Serve the Nasu Dengaku hot as a delicious appetizer or side dish.

Nasu Dengaku is a flavorful and satisfying dish that showcases the natural sweetness of eggplant combined with the savory umami flavors of miso glaze. Enjoy this classic Japanese dish as part of your next meal!

Ankake Yakisoba

Ingredients:

For the Yakisoba:

- 8 ounces (about 225g) yakisoba noodles (or substitute with ramen noodles)
- 2 tablespoons vegetable oil
- 1 small onion, thinly sliced
- 1 carrot, julienned
- 1 bell pepper, thinly sliced
- 1 cup cabbage, thinly sliced
- 4 ounces (about 115g) sliced pork or chicken (optional)
- 2 green onions, thinly sliced (for garnish)
- Toasted sesame seeds (for garnish)

For the Ankake Sauce:

- 1 cup dashi (Japanese soup stock)
- 2 tablespoons soy sauce
- 1 tablespoon mirin (Japanese sweet rice wine)
- 1 tablespoon oyster sauce
- 1 tablespoon cornstarch mixed with 2 tablespoons water (slurry)
- Salt and pepper, to taste

Instructions:

1. Cook the yakisoba noodles according to the package instructions. Drain and set aside.
2. In a small bowl, mix together the dashi, soy sauce, mirin, and oyster sauce to make the Ankake sauce. Set aside.
3. Heat 1 tablespoon of vegetable oil in a large skillet or wok over medium-high heat. Add the sliced pork or chicken (if using) and cook until browned and cooked through. Remove from the skillet and set aside.
4. In the same skillet, add another tablespoon of vegetable oil. Add the sliced onion, julienned carrot, thinly sliced bell pepper, and thinly sliced cabbage. Stir-fry for 2-3 minutes, or until the vegetables are slightly softened.

5. Add the cooked noodles and cooked meat (if using) back to the skillet with the vegetables.
6. Pour the Ankake sauce over the noodles and vegetables in the skillet. Stir well to combine and coat everything evenly with the sauce.
7. Cook for another 1-2 minutes, or until the sauce has thickened and the noodles are heated through.
8. Season with salt and pepper to taste, if needed.
9. Transfer the Ankake Yakisoba to serving plates or bowls.
10. Garnish with thinly sliced green onions and toasted sesame seeds.
11. Serve the Ankake Yakisoba hot and enjoy!

Ankake Yakisoba is a delicious and satisfying dish that combines tender noodles, flavorful sauce, and a variety of vegetables. Feel free to customize the ingredients and adjust the seasoning according to your taste preferences. Enjoy your homemade Ankake Yakisoba as a comforting and flavorful meal!

Kakiage Tempura Bowl

Ingredients:

For the Tempura:

- Assorted vegetables (such as onions, carrots, sweet potatoes, bell peppers, green beans, or shiitake mushrooms), thinly sliced or julienned
- 1 cup all-purpose flour
- 1/2 cup cornstarch
- 1 teaspoon baking powder
- 1 cup ice-cold water
- Vegetable oil, for frying
- Salt, to taste

For the Sauce:

- 1/2 cup dashi (Japanese soup stock)
- 2 tablespoons soy sauce
- 1 tablespoon mirin (Japanese sweet rice wine)
- 1 tablespoon sugar
- 1 teaspoon grated ginger (optional)
- 1 teaspoon grated daikon radish (optional)
- Thinly sliced green onions, for garnish

For Serving:

- Cooked Japanese short-grain rice

Instructions:

1. Prepare the vegetables by thinly slicing or julienning them into similar sizes.
2. In a mixing bowl, combine the all-purpose flour, cornstarch, baking powder, and ice-cold water. Stir until just combined; do not overmix. The batter should be lumpy and slightly thick.
3. Heat vegetable oil in a large pot or deep fryer to 350°F (180°C).

4. Dip the prepared vegetables into the tempura batter, shaking off any excess batter.
5. Carefully place the battered vegetables into the hot oil, frying in batches to avoid overcrowding the pot. Fry until the tempura is golden brown and crispy, about 2-3 minutes per batch. Remove with a slotted spoon and drain on paper towels. Season with salt while still hot.
6. In a small saucepan, combine the dashi, soy sauce, mirin, and sugar to make the sauce. Bring to a simmer over medium heat, stirring until the sugar is dissolved. Remove from heat and set aside.
7. To serve, divide the cooked Japanese short-grain rice among serving bowls.
8. Arrange the mixed vegetable tempura on top of the rice in each bowl.
9. Spoon the sauce over the tempura and rice.
10. Garnish with grated ginger, grated daikon radish, and thinly sliced green onions, if desired.
11. Serve the Kakiage Tempura Bowl immediately while the tempura is still crispy and hot.

Kakiage Tempura Bowl is a delicious and satisfying meal that's perfect for lunch or dinner. Enjoy the crispy texture of the tempura paired with the savory sauce and fluffy rice!

Tamago Sushi

Ingredients:

For the Tamago (Sweet Rolled Omelette):

- 4 large eggs
- 2 tablespoons granulated sugar
- 1 tablespoon mirin (Japanese sweet rice wine)
- 1 tablespoon soy sauce
- Vegetable oil, for greasing the pan

For the Sushi Rice:

- 1 cup sushi rice
- 1 1/4 cups water
- 2 tablespoons rice vinegar
- 1 tablespoon sugar
- 1/2 teaspoon salt

For Assembling the Tamago Sushi:

- Nori seaweed sheets, cut into strips (optional)
- Toasted sesame seeds (optional)
- Wasabi paste (optional)
- Soy sauce, for dipping

Instructions:

1. Rinse the sushi rice under cold water until the water runs clear. Drain well.
2. In a rice cooker or medium saucepan, combine the rinsed sushi rice and water. Cook according to the rice cooker's instructions or bring to a boil, then reduce heat to low, cover, and simmer for about 15-20 minutes, or until the rice is cooked and tender.
3. In a small saucepan, combine the rice vinegar, sugar, and salt. Heat over low heat, stirring until the sugar and salt are dissolved. Remove from heat and let cool.

4. Once the rice is cooked, transfer it to a large bowl and gently fold in the seasoned vinegar mixture, being careful not to crush the rice grains. Let the seasoned rice cool to room temperature.
5. While the rice is cooling, prepare the Tamago. In a mixing bowl, beat the eggs with sugar, mirin, and soy sauce until well combined.
6. Heat a non-stick square or rectangular frying pan over medium heat. Lightly grease the pan with vegetable oil.
7. Pour a thin layer of the egg mixture into the pan, tilting the pan to spread the mixture evenly. Cook until the bottom is set but the top is still slightly runny.
8. Using a spatula, gently roll up the cooked egg from one end of the pan to the other to form a log shape. Push the rolled egg to one end of the pan.
9. Grease the empty part of the pan with more oil and pour another thin layer of the egg mixture into the pan, making sure to lift the rolled egg slightly to let the new layer of egg mixture flow underneath. Cook until set but still slightly runny on top.
10. Roll up the cooked egg again to incorporate it into the previous roll. Repeat this process until all the egg mixture is used up and you have a thick, rolled omelette.
11. Once the Tamago is cooked, transfer it to a cutting board and let it cool slightly.
12. Slice the Tamago into thin slices.
13. To assemble the Tamago Sushi, place a sheet of nori seaweed on a sushi mat (if using) and place a small portion of seasoned rice on top, leaving a border along one edge.
14. Place a slice of Tamago on top of the rice.
15. Roll up the sushi using the sushi mat, applying gentle pressure to shape it into a tight roll.
16. Repeat the process with the remaining rice and Tamago slices.
17. If desired, sprinkle toasted sesame seeds over the rolled sushi.
18. Use a sharp knife to slice the Tamago Sushi roll into bite-sized pieces.
19. Serve the Tamago Sushi with wasabi paste, soy sauce, and pickled ginger on the side.
20. Enjoy your delicious homemade Tamago Sushi!

Tamago Sushi is a classic and flavorful sushi option, perfect for sushi lovers who enjoy the sweetness of the rolled omelette paired with seasoned rice. Feel free to customize your Tamago Sushi with additional fillings or toppings according to your taste preferences!

Tori Nanban Fried Chicken with Tartar Sauce

Ingredients:

For the Fried Chicken:

- 2 boneless, skinless chicken breasts
- Salt and pepper, to taste
- All-purpose flour, for dredging
- 2 eggs, beaten
- Panko breadcrumbs, for coating
- Vegetable oil, for frying

For the Tartar Sauce:

- 1/2 cup mayonnaise
- 2 tablespoons finely chopped pickles or cornichons
- 1 tablespoon finely chopped onion
- 1 tablespoon finely chopped fresh parsley
- 1 teaspoon Dijon mustard
- 1 teaspoon lemon juice
- Salt and pepper, to taste

For Serving:

- Cooked Japanese short-grain rice
- Shredded lettuce or cabbage (optional)
- Lemon wedges (optional)

Instructions:

1. Preheat vegetable oil in a deep fryer or large pot to 350°F (180°C).
2. While the oil is heating, prepare the chicken. Slice the chicken breasts into thin strips or bite-sized pieces. Season with salt and pepper.
3. Set up a breading station with three shallow dishes: one with all-purpose flour, one with beaten eggs, and one with panko breadcrumbs.

4. Dredge the chicken pieces in the flour, shaking off any excess. Dip them into the beaten eggs, then coat them evenly with panko breadcrumbs.
5. Once the oil is hot, carefully add the breaded chicken pieces in batches, making sure not to overcrowd the fryer. Fry until golden brown and cooked through, about 4-5 minutes per batch. Remove with a slotted spoon and drain on paper towels.
6. While the chicken is frying, prepare the tartar sauce. In a small bowl, mix together the mayonnaise, chopped pickles, chopped onion, chopped parsley, Dijon mustard, and lemon juice until well combined. Season with salt and pepper to taste.
7. Once all the chicken pieces are fried, serve them hot with the tartar sauce on the side for dipping.
8. Optionally, serve the Tori Nanban over cooked Japanese short-grain rice and shredded lettuce or cabbage.
9. Garnish with lemon wedges for squeezing over the chicken, if desired.
10. Enjoy your delicious homemade Tori Nanban Fried Chicken with Tartar Sauce!

Tori Nanban is a popular dish in Japan, known for its crispy fried chicken paired with tangy tartar sauce. It's perfect for a comforting meal any day of the week. Feel free to adjust the seasoning and customize the tartar sauce according to your taste preferences!

Hiya Yakko Chilled Tofu

Ingredients:

- 1 block (about 14 oz or 400g) silken tofu
- Soy sauce, for drizzling
- Grated ginger, for garnish
- Thinly sliced green onions, for garnish
- Toasted sesame seeds, for garnish
- Nori seaweed sheets, cut into thin strips (optional, for garnish)

Instructions:

1. Carefully remove the tofu from its packaging and drain any excess liquid.
2. Slice the tofu block into serving-sized pieces and arrange them on individual plates or a serving platter.
3. Drizzle soy sauce over the tofu slices, using as much or as little as you like.
4. Garnish the tofu with grated ginger, thinly sliced green onions, toasted sesame seeds, and nori seaweed strips (if using).
5. Serve the Hiya Yakko immediately, and enjoy!

Hiya Yakko is a simple and refreshing dish that's perfect for hot summer days. It's light, flavorful, and packed with protein. Feel free to adjust the garnishes and seasoning according to your taste preferences. Enjoy your homemade Hiya Yakko chilled tofu!

Shabu-Shabu Hot Pot

Ingredients:

For the Broth:

- 6 cups water
- 1 piece (about 2 inches) kombu (dried kelp)
- 4 dried shiitake mushrooms
- 1/2 onion, sliced
- 2 cloves garlic, smashed
- 1 tablespoon soy sauce
- 1 tablespoon mirin (Japanese sweet rice wine)
- Salt, to taste

For the Hot Pot:

- Assorted thinly sliced meats (such as beef, pork, or chicken)
- Assorted vegetables (such as napa cabbage, spinach, carrots, mushrooms, and green onions)
- Tofu, sliced
- Shrimp, peeled and deveined
- Udon noodles or glass noodles (optional)
- Dipping sauces (such as ponzu sauce, sesame sauce, or goma dare)
- Cooked rice

Instructions:

1. In a large pot, combine water, kombu, dried shiitake mushrooms, sliced onion, smashed garlic, soy sauce, and mirin to make the broth. Bring to a boil over medium heat, then reduce heat to low and simmer for about 30 minutes to 1 hour to infuse the flavors. Season with salt to taste.
2. While the broth is simmering, prepare the meats and vegetables by slicing them thinly. Arrange them on a platter or plate for easy access.
3. Once the broth is ready, set up a portable gas burner or induction cooker on the dining table. Place the pot of broth on the burner and bring it to a gentle simmer.

4. To cook the ingredients, each person uses chopsticks or a small strainer to dip the raw ingredients into the simmering broth to cook them. Swirl the ingredients in the broth for a few seconds until cooked to your desired doneness. This dipping and cooking method is where the name "Shabu-Shabu" comes from, as it mimics the sound of ingredients being swirled in the pot.
5. Once cooked, remove the ingredients from the pot and dip them into your choice of dipping sauce before eating.
6. You can also add udon noodles or glass noodles to the broth to cook and serve them alongside the meats and vegetables.
7. Enjoy the Shabu-Shabu hot pot with cooked rice on the side.

Shabu-Shabu is a fun and interactive meal that's perfect for gatherings with family and friends. Customize your hot pot with your favorite meats, vegetables, and dipping sauces for a delicious and satisfying dining experience!

Somen Noodle Salad

Ingredients:

For the Salad:

- 8 ounces (about 225g) somen noodles
- 1 cucumber, julienned
- 1 carrot, julienned
- 1/2 red bell pepper, julienned
- 2 green onions, thinly sliced
- 1/4 cup cilantro leaves, chopped (optional)
- Sesame seeds, for garnish

For the Dressing:

- 1/4 cup soy sauce
- 2 tablespoons rice vinegar
- 1 tablespoon sesame oil
- 1 tablespoon honey or sugar
- 1 teaspoon grated ginger
- 1 clove garlic, minced
- 1 tablespoon toasted sesame seeds
- Red pepper flakes, to taste (optional)

Instructions:

1. Cook the somen noodles according to the package instructions. Drain and rinse the noodles under cold water to stop the cooking process and cool them down. Drain well.
2. In a large mixing bowl, combine the cooked and cooled somen noodles with the julienned cucumber, carrot, red bell pepper, green onions, and cilantro leaves (if using). Toss gently to combine.
3. In a small bowl, whisk together the soy sauce, rice vinegar, sesame oil, honey or sugar, grated ginger, minced garlic, toasted sesame seeds, and red pepper flakes (if using), until well combined.

4. Pour the dressing over the somen noodle salad and toss until everything is evenly coated with the dressing.
5. Transfer the salad to a serving platter or individual plates.
6. Garnish the somen noodle salad with additional sesame seeds.
7. Serve the Somen Noodle Salad chilled, and enjoy!

Somen Noodle Salad is a light and refreshing dish that's perfect for picnics, potlucks, or as a side dish for any meal. Feel free to customize the salad with your favorite vegetables or add protein such as grilled chicken, shrimp, or tofu for a heartier version. Enjoy your delicious homemade Somen Noodle Salad!

Yudofu Hot Tofu

Ingredients:

- 1 block (about 14 oz or 400g) firm tofu
- 4 cups water
- 1 piece kombu (about 2 inches)
- Soy sauce, for dipping (optional)
- Grated ginger, for garnish (optional)
- Thinly sliced green onions, for garnish (optional)
- Bonito flakes (katsuobushi), for garnish (optional)

Instructions:

1. Cut the block of tofu into serving-sized pieces.
2. In a pot, combine the water and kombu and bring to a gentle simmer over medium-low heat. Let it simmer for about 10 minutes to infuse the water with the flavor of the kombu.
3. Remove the kombu from the pot and discard it.
4. Gently add the tofu pieces to the simmering water.
5. Let the tofu simmer in the water for about 5-7 minutes, or until heated through.
6. Once heated through, carefully remove the tofu from the pot using a slotted spoon or tofu skimmer, and transfer them to serving bowls.
7. Serve the Yudofu hot, accompanied by soy sauce for dipping if desired.
8. Optionally, garnish the Yudofu with grated ginger, thinly sliced green onions, and bonito flakes.
9. Enjoy your comforting and nourishing Yudofu hot tofu!

Yudofu is a simple and soothing dish that highlights the delicate flavor and texture of tofu. It's perfect for a light meal or as part of a traditional Japanese breakfast. Feel free to adjust the garnishes and serve with other accompaniments such as steamed rice or pickled vegetables according to your taste preferences.

Buta no Kakuni Braised Pork Belly

Ingredients:

- 1 lb (about 450g) pork belly, cut into bite-sized cubes
- 2 cups water
- 1/2 cup soy sauce
- 1/2 cup mirin (Japanese sweet rice wine)
- 1/4 cup sugar
- 2 cloves garlic, minced
- 1 knob ginger, sliced
- 2 green onions, chopped (white and green parts separated)
- 2 dried shiitake mushrooms
- 1 piece kombu (dried kelp)
- 1 star anise (optional)
- Hard-boiled eggs (optional, for serving)
- Steamed rice, for serving

Instructions:

1. In a large pot or Dutch oven, combine water, soy sauce, mirin, sugar, minced garlic, sliced ginger, and the white parts of the green onions. Add the dried shiitake mushrooms, kombu, and star anise (if using).
2. Bring the mixture to a boil over medium-high heat, then reduce the heat to low and let it simmer for a few minutes to allow the flavors to meld together.
3. Add the cubed pork belly to the pot, making sure the pieces are submerged in the liquid.
4. Cover the pot with a lid and let the pork belly simmer gently over low heat for about 2 to 2 1/2 hours, or until the pork is tender and easily pierced with a fork. Stir occasionally to ensure even cooking and prevent sticking.
5. Once the pork belly is tender, remove it from the pot and transfer it to a serving plate.
6. If using, peel the hard-boiled eggs and add them to the pot of braising liquid. Let them simmer for a few minutes to absorb the flavors.
7. Serve the Buta no Kakuni hot, garnished with the green parts of the chopped green onions.
8. Optionally, serve the braised pork belly with the soft-boiled eggs and steamed rice on the side.

9. Enjoy your delicious Buta no Kakuni Japanese braised pork belly!

Buta no Kakuni is a flavorful and comforting dish that's perfect for enjoying with steamed rice and other side dishes. The tender, melt-in-your-mouth pork belly pairs perfectly with the rich, savory-sweet braising liquid. Feel free to adjust the seasoning and add other ingredients according to your taste preferences.

Kabocha Korokke Pumpkin Croquettes

Ingredients:

- 1 small kabocha squash (about 2 pounds), peeled, seeded, and cut into chunks
- 1 tablespoon vegetable oil
- 1 small onion, finely chopped
- 2 cloves garlic, minced
- 1/2 teaspoon ground ginger
- Salt and pepper, to taste
- 2 cups mashed kabocha squash (from the cooked kabocha)
- 1 cup cooked and mashed potatoes
- 1/4 cup panko breadcrumbs, plus extra for coating
- 2 tablespoons flour
- 1 egg, beaten
- Vegetable oil, for frying

Instructions:

1. Place the kabocha squash chunks in a pot of boiling water and cook until tender, about 15-20 minutes. Drain well and mash the cooked kabocha squash until smooth. Measure out 2 cups of mashed kabocha squash and set aside.
2. In a skillet, heat 1 tablespoon of vegetable oil over medium heat. Add the chopped onion and sauté until translucent, about 5 minutes. Add the minced garlic and ground ginger, and cook for an additional 1-2 minutes, until fragrant. Season with salt and pepper to taste. Remove from heat and let cool slightly.
3. In a large mixing bowl, combine the mashed kabocha squash, cooked and mashed potatoes, sautéed onion mixture, 1/4 cup panko breadcrumbs, and flour. Mix until well combined.
4. Take a small portion of the mixture and shape it into a croquette (oval or round shape). Repeat with the remaining mixture.
5. Dip each croquette into the beaten egg, then coat evenly with panko breadcrumbs.
6. Heat vegetable oil in a deep frying pan or pot to 350°F (180°C). Carefully add the croquettes to the hot oil in batches, making sure not to overcrowd the pan. Fry until golden brown and crispy, about 3-4 minutes per side.
7. Use a slotted spoon to transfer the cooked croquettes to a plate lined with paper towels to drain excess oil.

8. Serve the Kabocha Korokke hot, garnished with a sprinkle of salt and any desired dipping sauce, such as tonkatsu sauce or Japanese mayonnaise.
9. Enjoy your delicious Kabocha Korokke Japanese pumpkin croquettes!

Kabocha Korokke is a delightful Japanese snack or appetizer, perfect for enjoying during the fall season when kabocha squash is in abundance. These crispy and creamy croquettes are sure to be a hit with your family and friends. Feel free to customize the recipe by adding your favorite seasonings or fillings.

Ochazuke Rice with Tea

Ingredients:

- Cooked Japanese short-grain rice
- Green tea (sencha or genmaicha)
- Hot water
- Toppings (choose from the options below):
    - Salted salmon (shiozake)
    - Grilled salmon (sake)
    - Pickled plum (umeboshi)
    - Wakame seaweed
    - Nori seaweed, shredded
    - Shredded shiso leaves
    - Bonito flakes (katsuobushi)
    - Toasted sesame seeds
    - Thinly sliced green onions

Instructions:

1. Prepare the toppings of your choice. If using salted salmon or grilled salmon, cook them beforehand according to your preferred method. If using pickled plum, remove the pit and cut it into smaller pieces.
2. Brew a cup of green tea using loose tea leaves or tea bags. Use about 1 teaspoon of tea leaves per cup of hot water. Allow the tea to steep for 2-3 minutes, then strain the tea leaves and set aside.
3. Place a serving of cooked Japanese short-grain rice in a bowl.
4. Pour the brewed green tea over the rice until it is partially submerged. Add more hot water if desired to achieve the desired consistency.
5. Add your choice of toppings to the rice and tea. You can arrange them neatly on top of the rice or mix them in.
6. Optionally, sprinkle toasted sesame seeds and thinly sliced green onions over the top for additional flavor and garnish.
7. Serve the Ochazuke immediately while warm.
8. Enjoy your comforting and nourishing Ochazuke Japanese rice with tea!

Ochazuke is a simple and versatile dish that can be customized with various toppings to suit your taste preferences. It's perfect for a light meal or as a comforting snack, especially on chilly days. Feel free to experiment with different combinations of toppings to create your own unique Ochazuke recipe.

Chuka Kurage Japanese Marinated Jellyfish Salad

Ingredients:

- 1 package (about 200g) chuka kurage (Japanese marinated jellyfish)
- 1/2 cucumber, thinly sliced
- 1 carrot, julienned
- 2 tablespoons rice vinegar
- 1 tablespoon soy sauce
- 1 tablespoon sesame oil
- 1 tablespoon sugar
- 1 teaspoon grated ginger
- 1 clove garlic, minced
- Toasted sesame seeds, for garnish
- Thinly sliced green onions, for garnish

Instructions:

1. Rinse the chuka kurage under cold water to remove excess marinade. Drain well and set aside.
2. In a small bowl, whisk together the rice vinegar, soy sauce, sesame oil, sugar, grated ginger, and minced garlic to make the dressing.
3. In a large mixing bowl, combine the sliced cucumber, julienned carrot, and drained chuka kurage.
4. Pour the dressing over the vegetables and jellyfish, and toss gently to coat everything evenly.
5. Cover the bowl and refrigerate the Chuka Kurage salad for at least 30 minutes to allow the flavors to meld together.
6. Once chilled, transfer the salad to a serving platter or individual bowls.
7. Garnish the Chuka Kurage salad with toasted sesame seeds and thinly sliced green onions.
8. Serve the salad cold as an appetizer or side dish.

Chuka Kurage is a refreshing and flavorful salad that's perfect for summer or as a light and healthy addition to any meal. Enjoy its unique texture and umami-rich flavor with the combination of vegetables and dressing. Adjust the seasoning and ingredients according to your taste preferences.

Kani Salad Crab Salad

Ingredients:

- 1 package (about 8 oz or 225g) imitation crab sticks (kanikama), shredded
- 1 cucumber, julienned
- 1 carrot, julienned
- 1/2 cup mayonnaise
- 1 tablespoon rice vinegar
- 1 teaspoon sugar
- Salt and pepper, to taste
- Sesame seeds, for garnish
- Thinly sliced green onions, for garnish

Instructions:

1. In a large mixing bowl, combine the shredded imitation crab sticks, julienned cucumber, and julienned carrot.
2. In a small bowl, whisk together the mayonnaise, rice vinegar, sugar, salt, and pepper to make the dressing.
3. Pour the dressing over the crab and vegetable mixture, and toss gently to coat everything evenly.
4. Cover the bowl and refrigerate the Kani Salad for at least 30 minutes to allow the flavors to meld together.
5. Once chilled, transfer the salad to a serving platter or individual bowls.
6. Garnish the Kani Salad with sesame seeds and thinly sliced green onions.
7. Serve the salad cold as an appetizer or side dish.

Kani Salad is a popular Japanese dish known for its refreshing taste and delightful combination of flavors and textures. Enjoy its creamy dressing, crunchy vegetables, and tender crab meat. Feel free to customize the salad with additional ingredients such as avocado, lettuce, or tobiko (flying fish roe) according to your taste preferences.

Age Dashi Tofu

Ingredients:

For the Dashi Broth:

- 2 cups water
- 1 piece kombu (about 2 inches)
- 1/4 cup bonito flakes (katsuobushi)
- 2 tablespoons soy sauce
- 1 tablespoon mirin (Japanese sweet rice wine)
- 1 tablespoon sake (Japanese rice wine)
- 1 teaspoon sugar

For the Fried Tofu:

- 1 block (about 14 oz or 400g) firm tofu, drained and cut into cubes
- Cornstarch, for dusting
- Vegetable oil, for frying

For Garnish (optional):

- Thinly sliced green onions
- Grated daikon radish
- Shredded nori seaweed
- Toasted sesame seeds

Instructions:

1. Start by preparing the dashi broth. In a small pot, combine the water and kombu and let it soak for about 30 minutes.
2. Place the pot over medium heat and slowly bring the water to a simmer. Just before it comes to a boil, remove the kombu from the pot.
3. Add the bonito flakes to the pot and simmer for another 1-2 minutes.
4. Strain the dashi broth through a fine-mesh sieve lined with cheesecloth or a paper towel to remove the bonito flakes. Return the strained broth to the pot.

5. Add soy sauce, mirin, sake, and sugar to the pot with the dashi broth. Stir to combine, then keep the broth warm over low heat.
6. Meanwhile, prepare the tofu. Drain the tofu and cut it into cubes. Pat the tofu cubes dry with paper towels to remove excess moisture.
7. Dust the tofu cubes lightly with cornstarch, shaking off any excess.
8. Heat vegetable oil in a deep fryer or large pot to 350°F (180°C).
9. Carefully add the tofu cubes to the hot oil in batches, making sure not to overcrowd the fryer. Fry until golden brown and crispy, about 3-4 minutes per batch.
10. Use a slotted spoon to transfer the fried tofu cubes to a plate lined with paper towels to drain excess oil.
11. To serve, place the fried tofu cubes in serving bowls and pour the warm dashi broth over them.
12. Garnish the Age Dashi Tofu with thinly sliced green onions, grated daikon radish, shredded nori seaweed, and toasted sesame seeds, if desired.
13. Serve the Age Dashi Tofu hot and enjoy!

Age Dashi Tofu is a delicious and comforting dish with crispy fried tofu soaked in a flavorful dashi broth. It's perfect as an appetizer or as part of a Japanese meal. Adjust the seasoning and garnishes according to your taste preferences.

Yaki Onigiri Grilled Rice Balls

Ingredients:

- Cooked Japanese short-grain rice
- Soy sauce
- Vegetable oil or sesame oil
- Optional fillings (such as grilled salmon, pickled plum, or cooked vegetables)

Instructions:

1. Prepare the rice: Cook Japanese short-grain rice according to package instructions and let it cool slightly until it's cool enough to handle.
2. Shape the rice balls: Moisten your hands with water to prevent the rice from sticking, then take a handful of cooked rice and shape it into a ball, about the size of your palm. You can also add a filling of your choice in the center of the rice ball, such as grilled salmon, pickled plum, or cooked vegetables.
3. Flatten the rice balls slightly to form discs or oval shapes, about 1 inch thick.
4. Brush the surface of the rice balls with soy sauce on both sides, ensuring they are evenly coated.
5. Heat a non-stick skillet or grill pan over medium heat and lightly grease it with vegetable oil or sesame oil.
6. Place the rice balls on the skillet and grill them for about 3-4 minutes on each side, or until they develop a crispy, golden-brown crust.
7. Once the rice balls are grilled to perfection, remove them from the skillet and let them cool slightly before serving.
8. Optionally, you can brush the grilled rice balls with additional soy sauce for extra flavor.
9. Serve the Yaki Onigiri hot as a delicious snack or side dish.

Yaki Onigiri is a versatile dish that can be enjoyed on its own or paired with various toppings and sauces. Get creative with your fillings and toppings to customize the flavors to your liking. Enjoy the crispy exterior and fluffy interior of these grilled rice balls!

Ebi Mayo Shrimp with Spicy Mayo

Ingredients:

For the Shrimp:

- 12 large shrimp, peeled and deveined, tails left on
- Salt and pepper, to taste
- 2 tablespoons cornstarch
- Vegetable oil, for frying

For the Spicy Mayo Sauce:

- 1/4 cup mayonnaise
- 1 tablespoon Sriracha sauce (adjust to taste for desired spiciness)
- 1 teaspoon soy sauce
- 1 teaspoon rice vinegar
- 1 teaspoon honey or sugar

For Garnish:

- Thinly sliced green onions
- Toasted sesame seeds
- Lemon wedges

Instructions:

1. Preheat vegetable oil in a deep fryer or large pot to 350°F (180°C).
2. Pat the peeled and deveined shrimp dry with paper towels. Season the shrimp with salt and pepper.
3. Lightly coat the seasoned shrimp with cornstarch, shaking off any excess.
4. Carefully add the shrimp to the hot oil in batches, making sure not to overcrowd the fryer. Fry until golden brown and crispy, about 2-3 minutes per batch. Remove the fried shrimp with a slotted spoon and drain on paper towels.
5. In a small bowl, mix together mayonnaise, Sriracha sauce, soy sauce, rice vinegar, and honey (or sugar) to make the spicy mayo sauce. Adjust the amount of Sriracha sauce to your desired level of spiciness.

6. Once all the shrimp are fried, toss them in the spicy mayo sauce until evenly coated.
7. Transfer the Ebi Mayo shrimp to a serving platter and garnish with thinly sliced green onions and toasted sesame seeds.
8. Serve the Ebi Mayo shrimp hot, accompanied by lemon wedges for squeezing over the shrimp.

Ebi Mayo is a popular Japanese appetizer known for its crispy shrimp coated in spicy mayo sauce. Enjoy the combination of crunchy exterior and creamy, tangy sauce. Serve it as an appetizer or as part of a meal. Adjust the spiciness of the sauce according to your preference. Enjoy your delicious homemade Ebi Mayo shrimp!

Hamachi Kama Grilled Yellowtail Collar

Ingredients:

- 2 Hamachi Kama (yellowtail collars)
- Salt
- Lemon wedges, for serving
- Soy sauce, for serving
- Wasabi, for serving (optional)
- Pickled ginger, for serving (optional)

Instructions:

1. Preheat your grill to medium-high heat.
2. Pat the Hamachi Kama dry with paper towels. Score the skin of the collars with a sharp knife to prevent curling while grilling. Season both sides of the collars generously with salt.
3. Place the Hamachi Kama on the grill, skin-side down. Grill for about 5-7 minutes on each side, or until the skin is crispy and the flesh is cooked through. You can also rotate the collars halfway through cooking for cross-hatch grill marks, if desired.
4. Once the Hamachi Kama is grilled to perfection and the flesh flakes easily with a fork, remove it from the grill.
5. Transfer the grilled Hamachi Kama to a serving platter. Squeeze fresh lemon juice over the top for extra flavor.
6. Serve the Grilled Hamachi Kama hot, accompanied by soy sauce for dipping. You can also serve it with wasabi and pickled ginger on the side for additional flavor.
7. Enjoy the succulent and flavorful Grilled Hamachi Kama as a delicious appetizer or main dish.

Grilled Hamachi Kama is a delightful delicacy with tender, juicy meat and crispy skin. It's a perfect dish to enjoy during a barbecue or as part of a Japanese-style meal. Adjust the seasoning and accompaniments according to your taste preferences.

Katsudon Pork Cutlet Rice Bowl

Ingredients:

For the Pork Cutlets (Tonkatsu):

- 4 boneless pork loin chops (about 1/2 inch thick)
- Salt and pepper, to taste
- All-purpose flour, for dredging
- 2 eggs, beaten
- Panko breadcrumbs, for coating
- Vegetable oil, for frying

For the Sauce:

- 2 cups dashi broth (or substitute with chicken or vegetable broth)
- 4 tablespoons soy sauce
- 2 tablespoons mirin (Japanese sweet rice wine)
- 2 tablespoons sugar
- 1 onion, thinly sliced

For Serving:

- Cooked Japanese short-grain rice
- 4 eggs, beaten (for topping)
- Thinly sliced green onions, for garnish
- Pickled ginger (optional), for garnish

Instructions:

1. Prepare the Tonkatsu (pork cutlets): Season the pork chops with salt and pepper on both sides. Dredge each pork chop in flour, shaking off any excess. Dip the floured pork chops in beaten eggs, then coat them evenly with panko breadcrumbs, pressing gently to adhere.
2. Heat vegetable oil in a large skillet or frying pan over medium heat. Fry the pork cutlets until golden brown and cooked through, about 4-5 minutes per side. Transfer the cooked pork cutlets to a plate lined with paper towels to drain excess oil. Set aside.

3. In the same skillet or frying pan, discard any excess oil, leaving about 1 tablespoon in the pan. Add the sliced onions and sauté until softened and translucent.
4. In a separate bowl, mix together dashi broth, soy sauce, mirin, and sugar to make the sauce. Pour the sauce over the sautéed onions in the skillet.
5. Bring the sauce to a simmer, then add the fried pork cutlets to the skillet. Simmer gently for a few minutes to allow the flavors to meld together and the pork cutlets to absorb some of the sauce.
6. Meanwhile, prepare the beaten eggs for topping. Pour the beaten eggs evenly over the pork cutlets and sauce in the skillet. Cover and cook for another 2-3 minutes, or until the eggs are set.
7. To serve, place a serving of cooked Japanese short-grain rice in each bowl. Top with one pork cutlet and a generous amount of sauce. Garnish with thinly sliced green onions and pickled ginger, if desired.
8. Enjoy your delicious homemade Katsudon Pork Cutlet Rice Bowl!

Katsudon is a comforting and satisfying dish that's perfect for lunch or dinner. The crispy pork cutlets, savory sauce, and fluffy rice make for a delicious combination. Adjust the seasoning and garnishes according to your taste preferences.

Tsukemono Japanese Pickles

Ingredients:

- Assorted vegetables (such as cucumber, daikon radish, carrots, cabbage, turnips, etc.)
- Salt
- Rice vinegar
- Sugar
- Water

Instructions:

1. Wash and prepare the vegetables: Peel and slice them into thin, uniform pieces or cut them into bite-sized pieces or sticks, depending on your preference. You can also leave some vegetables whole or slice them into rounds.
2. Sprinkle the sliced vegetables generously with salt and let them sit for about 30 minutes to draw out excess moisture. This step helps to remove bitterness and firm up the vegetables.
3. After 30 minutes, rinse the salted vegetables under cold water to remove the excess salt. Drain well and pat them dry with paper towels.
4. In a separate bowl, mix together equal parts rice vinegar and water, and add sugar to taste. Start with about 1 tablespoon of sugar per cup of vinegar and adjust according to your preference for sweetness.
5. Place the rinsed and dried vegetables in a clean, dry jar or container.
6. Pour the rice vinegar mixture over the vegetables, making sure they are completely submerged. You can add additional flavorings such as sliced ginger, garlic, or chili peppers if desired.
7. Cover the jar or container and refrigerate the Tsukemono for at least a few hours, preferably overnight, to allow the flavors to develop and the vegetables to pickle.
8. Once pickled to your liking, serve the Tsukemono as a side dish or accompaniment to Japanese meals.
9. Enjoy your homemade Tsukemono Japanese pickles!

Tsukemono can be made with a variety of vegetables and flavorings, so feel free to experiment with different combinations to suit your taste preferences. These pickles add a refreshing and crunchy element to meals and are often served alongside rice and other dishes in Japanese cuisine. Adjust the seasoning and pickling time according to your preference for flavor and texture.

Natto Fermented Soybeans

Ingredients:

- 2 cups soybeans
- Natto starter culture (available online or from Asian grocery stores)
- Water

Instructions:

1. Rinse the soybeans thoroughly under cold water and soak them in water overnight or for at least 8 hours.
2. After soaking, drain the soybeans and cook them in a pot with fresh water. Bring the water to a boil, then reduce the heat and simmer the soybeans for about 3-4 hours, or until they are soft and fully cooked. Make sure the beans are tender but not mushy.
3. Drain the cooked soybeans and let them cool to room temperature.
4. In a clean and sterilized container, mix the cooked soybeans with the natto starter culture according to the instructions on the package. Typically, you'll sprinkle the starter culture over the soybeans and gently mix it in.
5. Cover the container with a clean cloth or paper towel and secure it with a rubber band. Place the container in a warm and dark place, ideally around 100°F (37°C), to ferment. You can use a yogurt maker, dehydrator, or oven with a pilot light for this purpose.
6. Allow the soybeans to ferment for about 24-48 hours. Check the natto periodically to ensure that it's fermenting properly and has developed a slimy texture and characteristic aroma.
7. Once the natto is fermented to your liking, transfer it to the refrigerator to halt the fermentation process.
8. Serve the homemade natto as desired, typically with soy sauce, mustard, chopped green onions, and rice.

Homemade natto may have a slightly different texture and flavor compared to commercially available varieties, but it can be a rewarding and fun project for those interested in fermentation and traditional Japanese cuisine. Ensure proper hygiene and sanitation practices throughout the process to prevent contamination.

www.ingramcontent.com/pod-product-compliance
Lightning Source LLC
LaVergne TN
LVHW061945070526
838199LV00060B/3985